# 2
# american popular piano
# SKILLS

**Created by**
## Dr. Scott McBride Smith

**Series Composer**
## Christopher Norton

**Editor**
## Dr. Scott McBride Smith

**Associate Editor**
## Clarke MacIntosh

**Book Design & Engraving**
Andrew Jones

**Cover Design**
Wagner Design

# Introduction

Everyone agrees that Tiger Woods is one of the greatest golfers of all time. Some even think he is the best ever! He won the 1997 Masters Tournament when he was 21 years old, the youngest winner in history. He was also the youngest golfer to complete a career *Grand Slam*, winning all four major championships by the age of 25.

How did he do it? Let's see what he says.

> *From early childhood I dreamed of being the world's best golfer. I worked hard and applied my family's values to everything I did. Integrity, honesty, discipline, responsiblity and fun; I learned these values at home and in school, each one pushing me further toward my dream.*

Eldrick (Tiger) Woods
Letter from Tiger, Tiger Woods Foundation Website
http://www.twfound.org

> *The best way to achieve [a] goal is through sound fundamentals.*

Tiger Woods
*Golf Digest*, November 1998

What's your dream? Do you want to be one of the world's best musicians? play piano for your own enjoyment? or entertain your friends and family? No matter which, Tiger is right. Hard work, responsibility – and fun! – will be the keystones to your success.

In golf, the term "fundamentals" covers many things. In piano playing, we can break it down into three broad groupings.

- **Technic.** This is the ability to readily make the motions that create beautiful sounds. Dynamic control, tonal evenness and variety, and speed would fall into this category.

- **Sightreading.** You might also call these "quick learning" skills. Seeing patterns, noticing details, and playing without stopping – right away.

- **Listening.** This is perhaps the most important of all! If you can't hear the sounds of a piece in your mind before you play, you will never do a good job performing it. Psychologists call this "audiation".

Do you think practicing basic skills is boring? Get over it!

Your playing will never be as good or as enjoyable as you want it to be if your basic skills are not excellent. Every athlete – including Tiger – spends time on drills, exercises and warm-ups outside of the game. Pianists should, too. When your piano fundamentals become strong, you will learn everything more easily and perform more confidently.

This book is designed to help, but it won't work if you don't! Practice carefully and frequently. Spend some time every day on your basic skills and, who knows ... you may become the Tiger Woods of the piano.

**Library and Archives Canada Cataloguing in Publication**

Smith, Scott McBride

American popular piano [music] : skills / created by Scott McBride Smith ;
series composer, Christopher Norton ;
editor, Scott McBride Smith ; associate editor, Clarke MacIntosh.

To be complete in 11 volumes.
Contents: Preparatory level -- Level 1 -- Level 2.
Miscellaneous information: The series is organized in 11 levels, from preparatory to level 10, each including a repertoire album,
an etudes album, a skills book, and an instrumental backings compact disc.

ISBN 978-1-897379-22-6 (preparatory level).--ISBN 978-1-897379-23-3 (level 1).--
ISBN 978-1-897379-24-0 (level 2)

1. Piano--Studies and exercises. 2. Piano--Studies and exercises--Juvenile.
I. Norton, Christopher, 1953- II. MacIntosh, S. Clarke, 1959- III. Title.

MT225.S659 2007                    786.2'142                    C2007-905832-9

# LEVEL 2 SKILLS
# Table of Contents

# Unit One - Module One

## A. Brainthumpers

Practice daily.

1) Play while counting out loud.

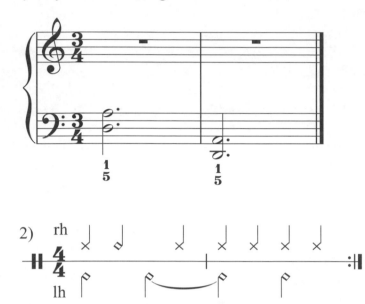

2)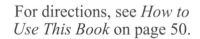

Tap this rhythmic pattern while counting out loud.
How many notes are in the left hand?_____

## B. Technic

Practice Daily.

For directions, see *How to Use This Book* on page 50.

1) Pentascales (pages 42-43)

No. _____; M.M. _____; key(s):  C  F  G

Articulation:  *legato  staccato  portato*

Dynamic:  *f  mf  mp*

2) Triads (pages 44-45)

No. _____; M.M. _____;  key(s):  C  F  G

Articulation:  *legato  staccato  portato*

Dynamic:  *f  mf  mp*

3) Scale Preparation (pages 46-49)

No. _____; M.M. _____; key:  C

Dynamic:  *f  mf  mp*

## C. Prepared Sightreading Piece

Play three times, keeping a steady beat.

For directions, see *How to Use This Book* on page 50.

## D. Aural Skills - Rhythmic

Practice daily.

1) ♩ = 60

   a) Clap 8 measures of ²⁄₄. Clap beat 1 with your hands in line with your left side, beat 2 with your hands in line with your right side.

   b) Count out loud as you clap. Beat 1 should be in a lower tone of voice, beat 2 in a higher.

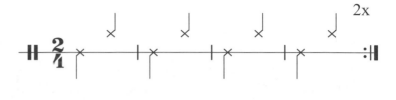

2) Study the musical example, below.

   a) Circle any note lengths in m. 3 that are different from m. 1.

   b) Clap the exercise while counting out loud. In m. 2, repeat the pattern from m. 1. In m. 4, repeat the pattern from m. 3.

   c) Now clap the whole pattern from memory.

## E. Aural Skills - Pitch

1) Play and sing a C Major pentascale up and down.

   a) Sing note E. You may have to silently sing the pentascale to yourself in order to locate the pitch.

   b) Sing down the pentascale from E to C.

2) Play a C Major triad.

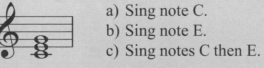

   a) Sing note C.
   b) Sing note E.
   c) Sing notes C then E.

3) Play the triad. Play the phrase at the piano and then sing it back without the piano. Sing it again from memory.

# Unit One - Module Two

## A. Brainthumpers

Practice daily.

1) Play the grace notes quickly.

2)

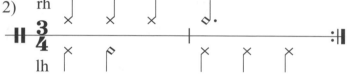

Tap this rhythmic pattern while counting out loud.
How many notes are in the left hand?_____

## B. Technic

Practice Daily.

For directions, see *How to Use This Book* on page 50.

1) Pentascales

No. _____; M.M. _____; key(s): C F G

Articulation: *legato staccato portato*

Dynamic: *f mf mp*

2) Triads

No. _____; M.M. _____; key(s): C F G

Articulation: *legato staccato portato*

Dynamic: *f mf mp*

3) Scale Preparation

No. _____; M.M. _____; key: C

Dynamic: *f mf mp*

## C. Prepared Sightreading Piece

Play three times, keeping a steady beat.

For directions, see *How to Use This Book* on page 50.

## D. Aural Skills - Rhythmic

Practice daily.

1) ♩ = 60

    a) Clap 9 measures of ¾. The beats should rise from lower left to upper right.

    b) Count out loud as you clap. Beat 1 should be in a lower tone of voice, beat 2 in the middle, and beat 3 higher.

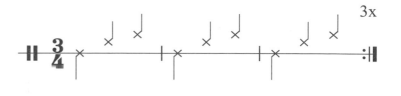

2) Study the musical example, below.

    a) Circle any note lengths in m. 3 that are different from m. 1.

    b) Clap the exercise while counting out loud. In m. 2, repeat the pattern from m. 1. In m. 4, repeat the pattern from m. 3.

    c) Now clap the whole pattern from memory.

## E. Aural Skills - Pitch

1) Play and sing a C Major pentascale up and down.

    a) Sing note G. You may have to silently sing the pentascale to yourself in order to locate the pitch.

    b) Sing down the pentascale from G to C.

2) Play a C Major triad.

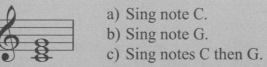

    a) Sing note C.

    b) Sing note G.

    c) Sing notes C then G.

3) Play the triad. Play the phrase at the piano and then sing it back without the piano. Sing it again from memory.

# Unit One - Module Three

## A. Brainthumpers

Practice daily.

1) Play while counting out loud.

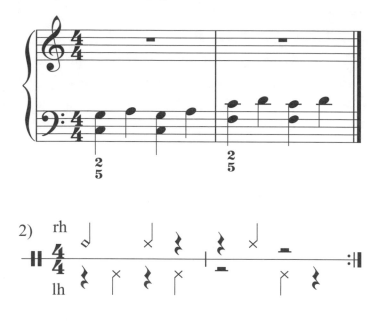

2) rh

Tap this rhythmic pattern while counting out loud.
How many notes are in the left hand?_____

## B. Technic

Practice Daily.
For directions, see *How to Use This Book* on page 50.

1) Pentascales

No. _____; M.M. _____; key(s):  C  F  G

Articulation:  *legato  staccato  portato*

Dynamic:  *f  mf  mp  ff*

2) Triads

No. _____; M.M. _____;  key(s):  C  F  G

Articulation:  *legato  staccato  portato*

Dynamic:  *f  mf  mp  ff*

3) Scale Preparation

No. _____; M.M. _____;  key:  C

Dynamic:  *f  mf  mp  ff*

## C. Prepared Sightreading Piece

Play three times, keeping a steady beat.

For directions, see *How to Use This Book* on page 50.

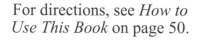

## D. Aural Skills - Rhythmic

Practice daily.

1) ♩ = 60

   a) Clap 8 measures of 4/4. The beats should rise
      from lower left to upper right.

   b) Count out loud as you clap. The voice should
      rise from beat 1 through to beat 4.

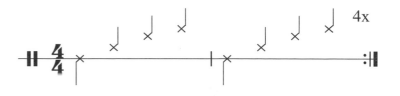

2) Study the musical example, below.

   a) Circle any note lengths in m. 3 that are different from m. 1.

   b) Clap the exercise while counting out loud. In m. 2, repeat
      the pattern from m. 1. In m. 4, repeat the pattern from m. 3.

   c) Now clap the whole pattern from memory.

## E. Aural Skills - Pitch

1) Play and sing a C Major pentascale up and down.

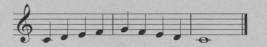

   a) Sing note D. You may have to silently sing the
      pentascale to yourself in order to locate the pitch.

   b) Sing down the pentascale from D to C.

2) Play a C Major triad.

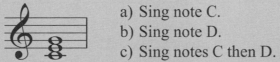

   a) Sing note C.
   b) Sing note D.
   c) Sing notes C then D.

3) Play the triad. Play the phrase at the piano and then sing it back without the piano.
   Sing it again from memory.

# Unit One - Module Four

## A. Brainthumpers

Practice daily.

1) Observe the slurs.

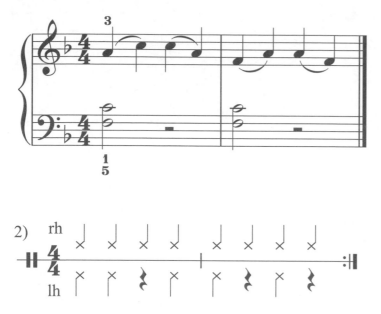

2) rh

Tap this rhythmic pattern while counting out loud.
How many notes are in the left hand? _____

## B. Technic

Practice Daily.
For directions, see *How to Use This Book* on page 50.

1) Pentascales

No. ____; M.M. ____; key(s): C F G

Articulation: *legato staccato portato*

Dynamic: ***f mf mp ff pp***

2) Triads

No. ____; M.M. ____; key(s): C F G

Articulation: *legato staccato portato*

Dynamic: ***f mf mp ff pp***

3) Scale Preparation

No. ____; M.M. ____; key: C

Dynamic: ***f mf mp ff pp***

## C. Prepared Sightreading Piece

Play three times, keeping a steady beat.

For directions, see *How to Use This Book* on page 50.

## D. Aural Skills - Rhythmic

Practice daily.

1) ♩ = 60

   a) Clap 9 measures of 3/4. The beats should rise from lower left to upper right.

   b) Count out loud as you clap. Beat 1 should be in a lower tone of voice, beat 2 in the middle, and beat 3 higher.

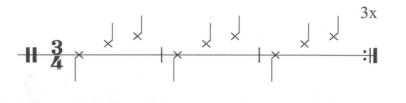

2) Study the musical example, below.

   a) Circle any note lengths in m. 3 that are different from m. 1.

   b) Clap the exercise while counting out loud. In m. 2, repeat the pattern from m. 1. In m. 4, repeat the pattern from m. 3.

   c) Now clap the whole pattern from memory.

## E. Aural Skills - Pitch

1) Play and sing a C Major pentascale up and down.

   a) Sing note F. You may have to silently sing the pentascale to yourself in order to locate the pitch.

   b) Sing down the pentascale from F to C.

2) Play a C Major triad.

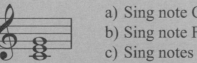

   a) Sing note C.
   b) Sing note F.
   c) Sing notes C then F.

3) Play the triad. Play the phrase at the piano and then sing it back without the piano. Sing it again from memory.

# Unit Two - Module One

## A. Brainthumpers

Practice daily.

1) Observe the fingering.

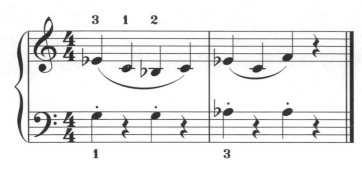

2)

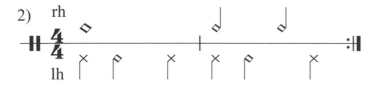

Tap this rhythmic pattern while counting out loud.
How many notes are in the left hand?_____

## B. Technic

Practice Daily.
For directions, see *How to Use This Book* on page 50.

1) Pentascales

No. ____; M.M. ____; key(s):  d  e  a

Articulation:  *legato  staccato  portato*

Dynamic:  **f  mf  mp**

2) Triads

No. ____; M.M. ____; key(s):  d  e  a

Articulation:  *legato  staccato  portato*

Dynamic:  **f  mf  mp**

3) Scale Preparation

No. ____; M.M. ____; key:  G

Dynamic:  **f  mf  mp**

## C. Prepared Sightreading Piece

Play three times, keeping a steady beat.

For directions, see *How to
Use This Book* on page 50.

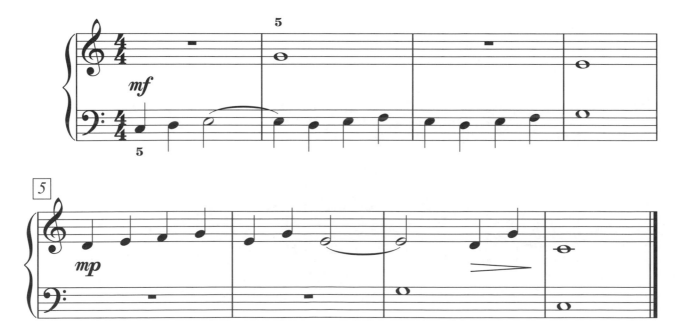

## D. Aural Skills - Rhythmic

Practice daily.

1) ♩ = 60

   a) Clap 8 measures of ²⁄₄. Clap beat 1 with your
      hands in line with your left side, beat 2 with
      your hands in line with your right side.

   b) Count out loud as you clap. Beat 1 should be
      in a lower tone of voice, beat 2 in a higher.

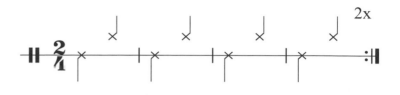

2) Study the musical example, below.

   a) Circle any note lengths in m. 3 that are different from m. 1.

   b) Clap the exercise while counting out loud. In m. 2, repeat
      the pattern from m. 1. In m. 4, repeat the pattern from m. 3.

   c) Now clap the whole pattern from memory.

## E. Aural Skills - Pitch

1) Play and sing a d minor pentascale up and down.

   a) Sing note G. You may have to silently sing the
      pentascale to yourself in order to locate the pitch.

   b) Sing down the pentascale from G to D.

2) Play a d minor triad.

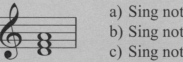

   a) Sing note D.
   b) Sing note G.
   c) Sing notes D then G.

3) Play the triad. Play the phrase at the piano and then sing it back without the piano.
   Sing it again from memory.

# Unit Two - Module Two

## A. Brainthumpers

Practice daily.

1) Observe the staccatos.

2)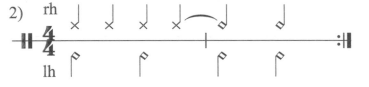

Tap this rhythmic pattern while counting out loud.
How many notes are in the left hand?_____

## B. Technic

Practice Daily.
For directions, see *How to Use This Book* on page 50.

1) Pentascales

No. ____; M.M. ____; key(s): d e a

Articulation: *legato staccato portato*

Dynamic: *f mf mp*

2) Triads

No. ____; M.M. ____; key(s): d e a

Articulation: *legato staccato portato*

Dynamic: *f mf mp*

3) Scale Preparation

No. ____; M.M. ____; key: G

Dynamic: *f mf mp*

## C. Prepared Sightreading Piece

Play three times, keeping a steady beat.

For directions, see *How to Use This Book* on page 50.

## D. Aural Skills - Rhythmic

Practice daily.

1) ♩ = 60

   a) Clap 8 measures of $\frac{4}{4}$. The beats should rise
      from lower left to upper right.

   b) Count out loud as you clap. The voice should
      rise from beat 1 through to beat 4.

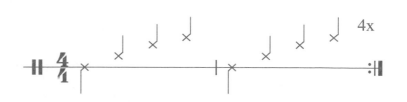

2) Study the musical example, below.

   a) Circle any note lengths in m. 3 that are different from m. 1.

   b) Clap the exercise while counting out loud. In m. 2, repeat
      the pattern from m. 1. In m. 4, repeat the pattern from m. 3.

   c) Now clap the whole pattern from memory.

## E. Aural Skills - Pitch

1) Play and sing a d minor pentascale up and down.

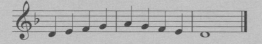

   a) Sing note A. You may have to silently sing the
      pentascale to yourself in order to locate the pitch.

   b) Sing down the pentascale from A to D.

2) Play a d minor triad.

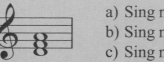

   a) Sing note D.
   b) Sing note A.
   c) Sing notes D then A.

3) Play the triad. Play the phrase at the piano and then sing it back without the piano.
   Sing it again from memory.

# Unit Two - Module Three

## A. Brainthumpers

Practice daily.

1) Observe the right hand slurs.

2)

Tap this rhythmic pattern while counting out loud.
How many notes are in the left hand?_____

## B. Technic

Practice Daily.
For directions, see *How to Use This Book* on page 50.

1) Pentascales

No. _____; M.M. _____; key(s): d  e  a

Articulation: *legato  staccato  portato*

Dynamic: ***f  mf  mp  ff***

2) Triads

No. _____; M.M. _____; key(s): d  e  a

Articulation: *legato  staccato  portato*

Dynamic: ***f  mf  mp  ff***

3) Scale Preparation

No. _____; M.M. _____; key:  G

Dynamic: ***f  mf  mp  ff***

## C. Prepared Sightreading Piece

Play three times, keeping a steady beat.

For directions, see *How to Use This Book* on page 50.

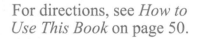

## D. Aural Skills - Rhythmic

Practice daily.

1)  ♩ = 60

   a) Clap 9 measures of $\frac{3}{4}$.  The beats should rise
      from lower left to upper right.

   b) Count out loud as you clap.  Beat 1 should be
      in a lower tone of voice, beat 2 in the middle,
      and beat 3 higher.

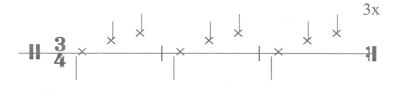

2) Study the musical example, below.

   a) Circle any note lengths in m. 3 that are different from m. 1.

   b) Clap the exercise while counting out loud.  In m. 2, repeat
      the pattern from m. 1.  In m. 4, repeat the pattern from m. 3.

   c) Now clap the whole pattern from memory.

## E. Aural Skills - Pitch

1) Play and sing a d minor pentascale up and down.

   a) Sing note F.  You may have to silently sing the
      pentascale to yourself in order to locate the pitch.

   b) Sing down the pentascale from F to D.

2) Play a d minor triad.

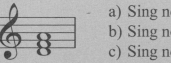

   a) Sing note D.
   b) Sing note F.
   c) Sing notes D then F.

3) Play the triad.  Play the phrase at the piano and then sing it back without the piano.
   Sing it again from memory.

# Unit Two - Module Four

16

## A. Brainthumpers

Practice daily.

1) Observe the slurs.

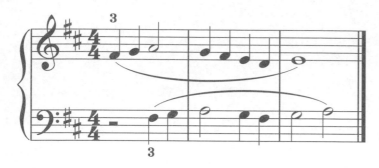

2)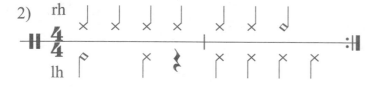

Tap this rhythmic pattern while counting out loud.
How many notes are in the left hand?_____

**B. Technic**

Practice Daily.
For directions, see *How to Use This Book* on page 50.

1) Pentascales

No. ____; M.M. ____; key(s): d e a

Articulation: *legato staccato portato*

Dynamic: *f mf mp ff pp*

2) Triads

No. ____; M.M. ____; key(s): d e a

Articulation: *legato staccato portato*

Dynamic: *f mf mp ff pp*

3) Scale Preparation

No. ____; M.M. ____; key: G

Dynamic: *f mf mp ff pp*

## C. Prepared Sightreading Piece

Play three times, keeping a steady beat.

For directions, see *How to Use This Book* on page 50.

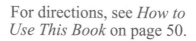

## D. Aural Skills - Rhythmic

Practice daily.

1) ♩ = 60

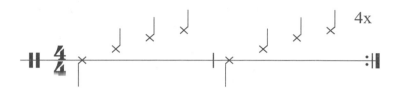

   a)  Clap 8 measures of 4/4. The beats should rise
       from lower left to upper right.

   b)  Count out loud as you clap. The voice should
       rise from beat 1 through to beat 4.

2) Study the musical example, below.

   a)  Circle any note lengths in m. 3 that are different from m. 1.

   b)  Clap the exercise while counting out loud. In m. 2, repeat
       the pattern from m. 1. In m. 4, repeat the pattern from m. 3.

   c)  Now clap the whole pattern from memory.

## E. Aural Skills - Pitch

1) Play and sing a d minor pentascale up and down.

   a) Sing note E. You may have to silently sing the
      pentascale to yourself in order to locate the pitch.

   b) Sing down the pentascale from E to D.

2) Play a d minor triad.

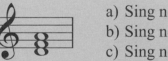

   a) Sing note D.
   b) Sing note E.
   c) Sing notes D then E.

3) Play the triad. Play the phrase at the piano and then sing it back without the piano.
   Sing it again from memory.

# Unit Three - Module Two

## A. Brainthumpers

Practice daily.

1) Play while counting out loud.

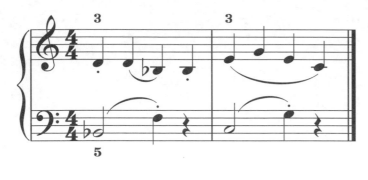

## B. Technic

Practice Daily.

For directions, see *How to Use This Book* on page 50.

1) Pentascales

No. _____; M.M. _____; key(s): D E A

Articulation: *legato staccato portato*

Dynamic: ***f*** *mf* *mp*

2) Triads

No. _____; M.M. _____; key(s): D E A

Articulation: *legato staccato portato*

Dynamic: ***f*** *mf* *mp*

3) Scale Preparation

No. _____; M.M. _____; key: D

Dynamic: ***f*** *mf* *mp*

2)

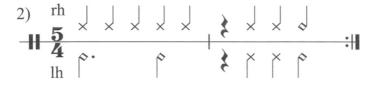

Tap this rhythmic pattern while counting out loud.
How many notes are in the right hand?_____

## C. Prepared Sightreading Piece

Play three times, keeping a steady beat.

For directions, see *How to Use This Book* on page 50.

## D. Aural Skills - Rhythmic

Practice daily.

1) Imagine three points in the air, the second higher
   than the first and the third higher than the second.

   Count 8 measures of ¾. Point to the lower dot as
   you say "one", to the middle dot as you say "two",
   and to the highest dot as you say "three".

   Say beat 1 more loudly than beats 2 and 3.

2) Study the musical example, below.

   a)  Circle any note lengths in m. 3 that are different from m. 1.

   b)  Clap the exercise while counting out loud. In m. 2, repeat
       the pattern from m. 1. In m. 4, repeat the pattern from m. 3.

   c)  Now clap the whole pattern from memory.

## E. Aural Skills - Pitch

1) Play and sing a D Major pentascale up and down.

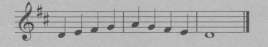

   a) Sing note G. You may have to silently sing the
      pentascale to yourself in order to locate the pitch.

   b) Sing down the pentascale from G to D.

2) Play a D Major triad.

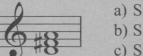

   a) Sing note D.
   b) Sing note G.
   c) Sing notes D then G.

3) Play the triad. Play the phrase at the piano and then sing it back without the piano.
   Sing it again from memory.

# Unit Three - Module Three

## A. Brainthumpers

Practice daily.

1) Play while counting out loud.

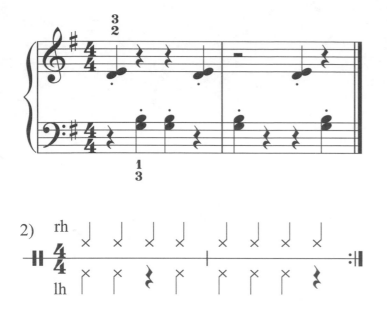

2) rh

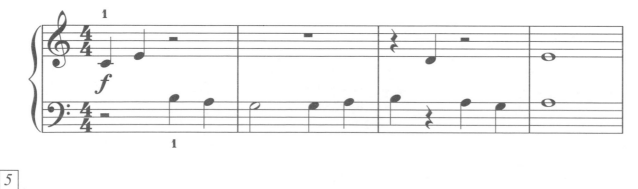

lh

Tap this rhythmic pattern while counting out loud.
How many notes are in the right hand?_____

## B. Technic

Practice Daily.

For directions, see *How to Use This Book* on page 50.

1) Pentascales

No. _____; M.M. _____; key(s): D  E  A

Articulation: *legato  staccato  portato*

Dynamic: *f  mf  mp  ff*

2) Triads

No. _____; M.M. _____; key(s): D  E  A

Articulation: *legato  staccato  portato*

Dynamic: *f  mf  mp  ff*

3) Scale Preparation

No. _____; M.M. _____; key: D

Dynamic: *f  mf  mp  ff*

## C. Prepared Sightreading Piece

Play three times, keeping a steady beat.

For directions, see *How to Use This Book* on page 50.

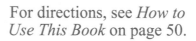

## D.  Aural Skills - Rhythmic

Practice daily.

1)  Imagine four points in the air, each one higher than
    the one before.

    Count 8 measures of ⁴⁄₄.  Point to the lowest dot as
    you say "one", and to each following dot as you say
    "two", "three", and "four".

    Say beat 1 more loudly than beat 2 and beat 3
    louder than beat 4, but not as loud as beat 1.

2)  Study the musical example, below.

    a)  Circle any note lengths in m. 3 that are different from m. 1.

    b)  Clap the exercise while counting out loud.  In m. 2, repeat
        the pattern from m. 1.  In m. 4, repeat the pattern from m. 3.

    c)  Now clap the whole pattern from memory.

## E.  Aural Skills - Pitch

1)  Play and sing a D Major pentascale up and down.

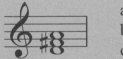

    a) Sing note E.  You may have to silently sing the
       pentascale to yourself in order to locate the pitch.

    b) Sing down the pentascale from E to D.

2)  Play a D Major triad.

    a) Sing note D.
    b) Sing note E.
    c) Sing notes D then E.

3)  Play the triad.  Play the phrase at the piano and then sing it back without the piano.
    Sing it again from memory.

# Unit Three - Module Four

## A. Brainthumpers

Practice daily.

1) Hold each note for full value.

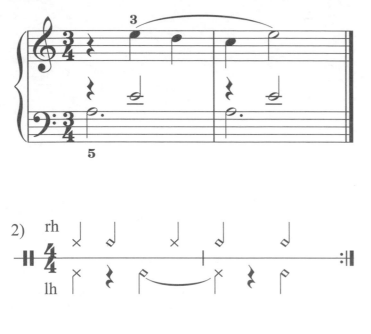

2) rh

Tap this rhythmic pattern while counting out loud.
How many notes are in the right hand?_____

## B. Technic

Practice Daily.

For directions, see *How to Use This Book* on page 50.

1) Pentascales

No. ____; M.M. ____; key(s): D  E  A

Articulation: *legato  staccato  portato*

Dynamic: *f  mf  mp  ff  pp*

2) Triads

No. ____; M.M. ____; key(s): D  E  A

Articulation: *legato  staccato  portato*

Dynamic: *f  mf  mp  ff  pp*

3) Scale Preparation

No. ____; M.M. ____; key: D

Dynamic: *f  mf  mp  ff  pp*

## C. Prepared Sightreading Piece

Play three times, keeping a steady beat.

For directions, see *How to Use This Book* on page 50.

## D. Aural Skills - Rhythmic

Practice daily.

1) Imagine three points in the air, the second higher than the first and the third higher than the second.

   Count 8 measures of ¾. Point to the lower dot as you say "one", to the middle dot as you say "two", and to the highest dot as you say "three".

   Say beat 1 more loudly than beats 2 and 3.

4x

2) Study the musical example, below.

   a) Circle any note lengths in m. 3 that are different from m. 1.

   b) Clap the exercise while counting out loud. In m. 2, repeat the pattern from m. 1. In m. 4, repeat the pattern from m. 3.

   c) Now clap the whole pattern from memory.

## E. Aural Skills - Pitch

1) Play and sing a D Major pentascale up and down.

   a) Sing note A. You may have to silently sing the pentascale to yourself in order to locate the pitch.

   b) Sing down the pentascale from A to D.

   2) Play a D Major triad.

   a) Sing note D.
   b) Sing note A.
   c) Sing notes D then A.

3) Play the triad. Play the phrase at the piano and then sing it back without the piano. Sing it again from memory.

# Unit Four - Module One

## A. Brainthumpers

Practice daily.

1) Play the grace note quickly.

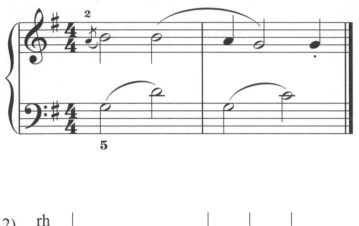

2)

Tap this rhythmic pattern while counting out loud.
How many notes are in the right hand?_____

## B. Technic

Practice Daily.

For directions, see *How to Use This Book* on page 50.

1) Pentascales

No. ____ ; M.M. ____ ; key(s):  c  f  g

Articulation:  *legato  staccato  portato*

Dynamic:  *f  mf  mp*

2) Triads

No. ____ ; M.M. ____ ; key(s):  c  f  g

Articulation:  *legato  staccato  portato*

Dynamic:  *f  mf  mp*

3) Scale Preparation

No. ____ ; M.M. ____ ; key:  C  G  D

Dynamic:  *f  mf  mp  ff  pp*

## C.  Prepared Sightreading Piece

Play three times, keeping a steady beat.

For directions, see *How to Use This Book* on page 50.

## D. Aural Skills - Rhythmic

Practice daily.

1) Imagine four points in the air, each one higher than the one before.

   Count 8 measures of $\frac{4}{4}$. Point to the lowest dot as you say "one", and to each following dot as you say "two", "three", and "four".

   Say beat 1 more loudly than beat 2 and beat 3 louder than beat 4, but not as loud as beat 1.

2) Study the musical example, below.

   a) Circle any note lengths in m. 3 that are different from m. 1.

   b) Clap the exercise while counting out loud. In m. 2, repeat the pattern from m. 1. In m. 4, repeat the pattern from m. 3.

   c) Now clap the whole pattern from memory.

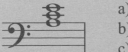

## E. Aural Skills - Pitch

1) Play and sing an a minor pentascale up and down.

   a) Sing note C. You may have to silently sing the pentascale to yourself in order to locate the pitch.

   b) Sing down the pentascale from C to A.

2) Play an a minor triad.

   a) Sing note A.
   b) Sing note C.
   c) Sing notes A then C.

3) Play the triad. Play the phrase at the piano and then sing it back without the piano. Sing it again from memory.

# Unit Four - Module Two

## A. Brainthumpers

Practice daily.

1) Play while counting out loud.

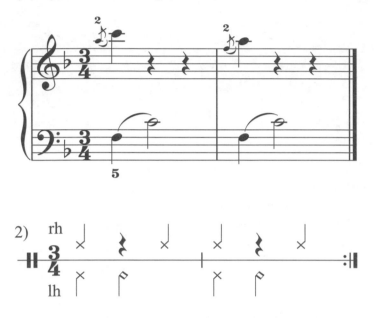

2)

Tap this rhythmic pattern while counting out loud.
How many notes are in the right hand?_____

## B. Technic

Practice Daily.
For directions, see *How to Use This Book* on page 50.

1) Pentascales

   No. _____; M.M. _____; key(s):  c  f  g

   Articulation:  *legato  staccato  portato*

   Dynamic:  *f  mf  mp*

2) Triads

   No. _____; M.M. _____; key(s):  c  f  g

   Articulation:  *legato  staccato  portato*

   Dynamic:  *f  mf  mp*

3) Scale Preparation

   No. _____; M.M. _____; key:  C  G  D

   Dynamic:  *f  mf  mp  ff  pp*

## C. Prepared Sightreading Piece

Play three times, keeping a steady beat.

For directions, see *How to Use This Book* on page 50.

## D. Aural Skills - Rhythmic

Practice daily.

1) Imagine two points in the air, the second higher than the first.

   Count 8 measures of $\frac{2}{4}$.  Point to the lower dot as you say "one", to the higher dot as you say "two".

   Say beat 1 more loudly than beat 2.

2) Study the musical example, below.

   a)  Circle any note lengths in m. 3 that are different from m. 1.

   b)  Clap the exercise while counting out loud.  In m. 2, repeat the pattern from m. 1.  In m. 4, repeat the pattern from m. 3.

   c)  Now clap the whole pattern from memory.

## E. Aural Skills - Pitch

1)  Play and sing an a minor pentascale up and down.

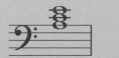

a) Sing note E.  You may have to silently sing the pentascale to yourself in order to locate the pitch.

b) Sing down the pentascale from E to A.

2)  Play an a minor triad.

a) Sing note A.
b) Sing note E.
c) Sing notes A then E.

3)  Play the triad.  Play the phrase at the piano and then sing it back without the piano. Sing it again from memory.

# Unit Four - Module Four

## A. Brainthumpers

Practice daily.

1) Observe the fingering.

2) rh

lh

Tap this rhythmic pattern while counting out loud.
How many notes are in the right hand?_____

## B. Technic

Practice Daily.

For directions, see *How to Use This Book* on page 50.

1) Pentascales

No. ____; M.M. ____; key(s): c f g

Articulation: *legato staccato portato*

Dynamic: *f mf mp ff pp*

2) Triads

No. ____; M.M. ____; key(s): c f g

Articulation: *legato staccato portato*

Dynamic: *f mf mp ff pp*

3) Scale Preparation

No. ____; M.M. ____; key: C G D

Dynamic: *f mf mp ff pp*

## C. Prepared Sightreading Piece

Play three times, keeping a steady beat.

For directions, see *How to Use This Book* on page 50.

## D. Aural Skills - Rhythmic

Practice daily.

1) Imagine four points in the air, each one higher than the one before.

Count 8 measures of ⁴⁄₄. Point to the lowest dot as you say "one", and to each following dot as you say "two", "three", and "four".

Say beat 1 more loudly than beat 2 and beat 3 louder than beat 4, but not as loud as beat 1.

2) Study the musical example, below.

   a) Circle any note lengths in m. 3 that are different from m. 1.

   b) Clap the exercise while counting out loud. In m. 2, repeat the pattern from m. 1. In m. 4, repeat the pattern from m. 3.

   c) Now clap the whole pattern from memory.

## E. Aural Skills - Pitch

1) Play and sing an a minor pentascale up and down.

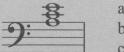

   a) Sing note D. You may have to silently sing the pentascale to yourself in order to locate the pitch.

   b) Sing down the pentascale from D to A.

2) Play an a minor triad.

   a) Sing note A.
   b) Sing note D.
   c) Sing notes A then D.

3) Play the triad. Play the phrase at the piano and then sing it back without the piano. Sing it again from memory.

# Unit 1 - Midterm

**I. Technic** Grade [ ]

Student to play pentascale:

No(s). _____; key(s) _____; M.M. _____;

Articulation _____; Dynamic(s) _____

Student to play triad:

No(s). _____; key(s) _____; M.M. _____;

Articulation _____; Dynamic(s) _____

**II. Sightreading** Grade [ ] Student may study for up to 15 seconds.

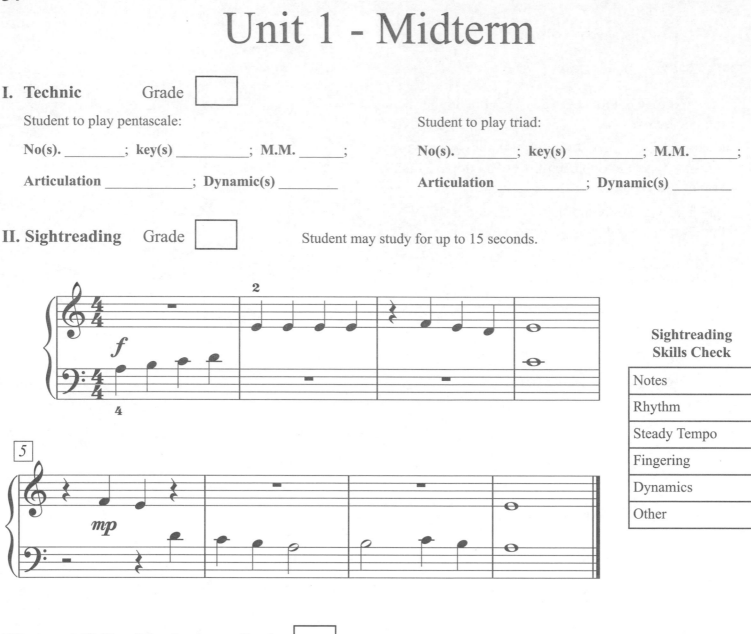

**Sightreading Skills Check**

| Notes |
| --- |
| Rhythm |
| Steady Tempo |
| Fingering |
| Dynamics |
| Other |

**III. Aural Skills - Rhythmic** Grade [ ]

Each element may be done twice.

**A. Echo Clap**

Alternating clap. Ask student to echo your m.1 in m. 2, and m. 3 in m. 4.

**B. Beat Clap-Along**

Tell the student you will be playing in $\frac{2}{4}$ time. Ask them to clap the ♩ beat as you play, joining in after a few beats. Beat 1 should align with the left side of their body, beat 2 with the right. Play *After Beyer* (*APP* Etudes Album 2, p. 56).

**IV. Aural Skills - Pitch** Grade [ ]

Each element may be done twice.

**A. Echo Sing**

Play a C Major triad. Play the phrase at the piano. Ask the student to sing it back without the piano.

**B. Interval-Sing**

1. Play a C Major pentascale. Ask the student to sing along with the piano.
2. Ask the student to sing note D. Ask them to sing down the notes of the pentascale from D to C.
3. Play a C Major triad. Ask the student to sing E then sing G.

# Unit 1 - Final

**I. Technic**     Grade ☐

Student to play pentascale:

No(s). _____ ; key(s) _____ ; M.M. _____ ;          No(s). _____ ; key(s) _____ ; M.M. _____ ;

Articulation _____ ; Dynamic(s) _____          Articulation _____ ; Dynamic(s) _____

**II. Sightreading**     Grade ☐          Student may study for up to 15 seconds.

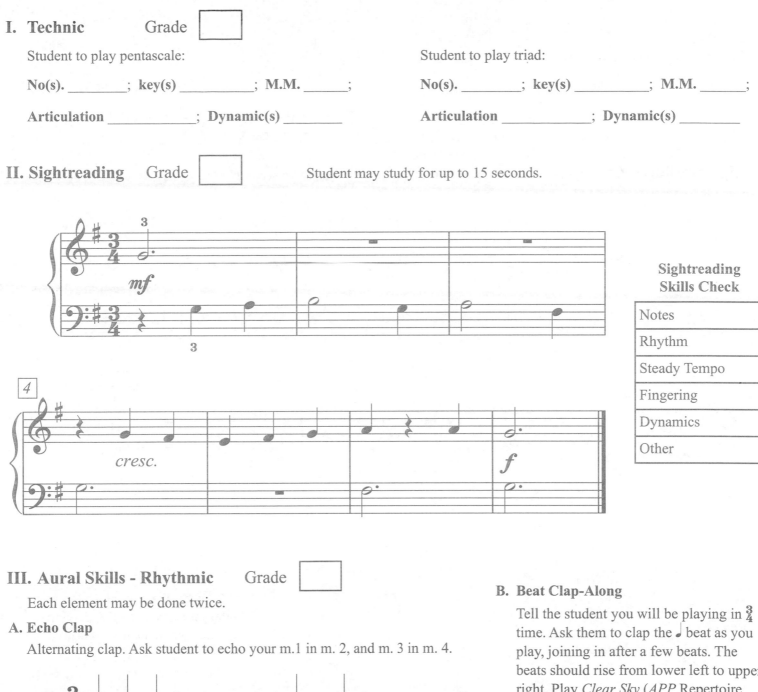

**Sightreading Skills Check**

| Notes |
|---|
| Rhythm |
| Steady Tempo |
| Fingering |
| Dynamics |
| Other |

**III. Aural Skills - Rhythmic**     Grade ☐

Each element may be done twice.

**A. Echo Clap**

Alternating clap. Ask student to echo your m.1 in m. 2, and m. 3 in m. 4.

**B. Beat Clap-Along**

Tell the student you will be playing in $\frac{3}{4}$ time. Ask them to clap the ♩ beat as you play, joining in after a few beats. The beats should rise from lower left to upper right. Play *Clear Sky* (*APP* Repertoire Album 2, p. 8).

**IV. Aural Skills - Pitch**     Grade ☐

Each element may be done twice.

**A. Echo Sing**

Play a C Major triad. Play the phrase at the piano. Ask the student to sing it back without the piano.

**B. Interval-Sing**

1. Play a C Major pentascale. Ask the student to sing along with the piano.
2. Ask the student to sing note E. Ask them to sing down the notes of the pentascale from E to C.
3. Play a C Major triad. Ask the student to sing G then sing C.

# Unit 2 - Midterm

**I. Technic**     Grade   ☐

Student to play pentascale:           Student to play triad:

No(s). _____ ; key(s) _____ ; M.M. _____ ;     No(s). _____ ; key(s) _____ ; M.M. _____ ;

Articulation _____ ; Dynamic(s) _____     Articulation _____ ; Dynamic(s) _____

**II. Sightreading**    Grade   ☐     Student may study for up to 15 seconds.

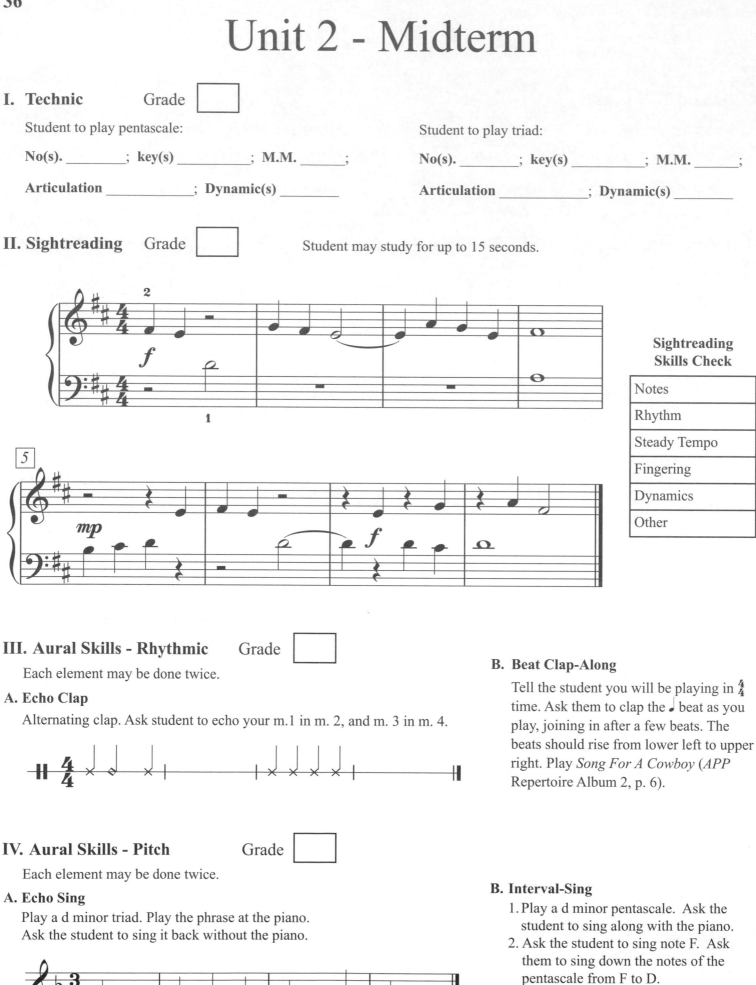

**Sightreading Skills Check**

| |
|---|
| Notes |
| Rhythm |
| Steady Tempo |
| Fingering |
| Dynamics |
| Other |

**III. Aural Skills - Rhythmic**    Grade   ☐

Each element may be done twice.

**A. Echo Clap**

Alternating clap. Ask student to echo your m.1 in m. 2, and m. 3 in m. 4.

**B. Beat Clap-Along**

Tell the student you will be playing in 4/4 time. Ask them to clap the ♩ beat as you play, joining in after a few beats. The beats should rise from lower left to upper right. Play *Song For A Cowboy* (*APP* Repertoire Album 2, p. 6).

**IV. Aural Skills - Pitch**    Grade   ☐

Each element may be done twice.

**A. Echo Sing**

Play a d minor triad. Play the phrase at the piano. Ask the student to sing it back without the piano.

**B. Interval-Sing**

1. Play a d minor pentascale. Ask the student to sing along with the piano.
2. Ask the student to sing note F. Ask them to sing down the notes of the pentascale from F to D.
3. Play a d minor triad. Ask the student to sing D then sing F.

# Unit 2 - Final

**I. Technic**     Grade [ ]

Student to play pentascale:                 Student to play triad:

No(s). _____ ; key(s) _____ ; M.M. _____ ;    No(s). _____ ; key(s) _____ ; M.M. _____ ;

Articulation _____ ; Dynamic(s) _____      Articulation _____ ; Dynamic(s) _____

**II. Sightreading**     Grade [ ]      Student may study for up to 15 seconds.

**Sightreading
Skills Check**

| Notes |
| Rhythm |
| Steady Tempo |
| Fingering |
| Dynamics |
| Other |

**III. Aural Skills - Rhythmic**     Grade [ ]

Each element may be done twice.

**A. Echo Clap**

Alternating clap. Ask student to echo your m.1 in m. 2, and m. 3 in m. 4.

**B. Beat Clap-Along**

Tell the student you will be playing in ¾ time. Ask them to clap the ♩ beat as you play, joining in after a few beats. The beats should rise from lower left to upper right. Play *Oscillations* (*APP* Etudes Album 2, p. 67).

**IV. Aural Skills - Pitch**     Grade [ ]

Each element may be done twice.

**A. Echo Sing**

Play a d minor triad. Play the phrase at the piano. Ask the student to sing it back without the piano.

**B. Interval-Sing**

1. Play a d minor pentascale. Ask the student to sing along with the piano.
2. Ask the student to sing note G. Ask them to sing down the notes of the pentascale from G to D.
3. Play a d minor triad. Ask the student to sing D then sing A.

# Unit 3 - Midterm

**I. Technic**    Grade [ ]

Student to play pentascale:

No(s). _____; key(s) _____; **M.M.** _____;

**Articulation** _____; **Dynamic(s)** _____

Student to play triad:

No(s). _____; key(s) _____; **M.M.** _____;

**Articulation** _____; **Dynamic(s)** _____

**II. Sightreading**    Grade [ ]    Student may study for up to 15 seconds.

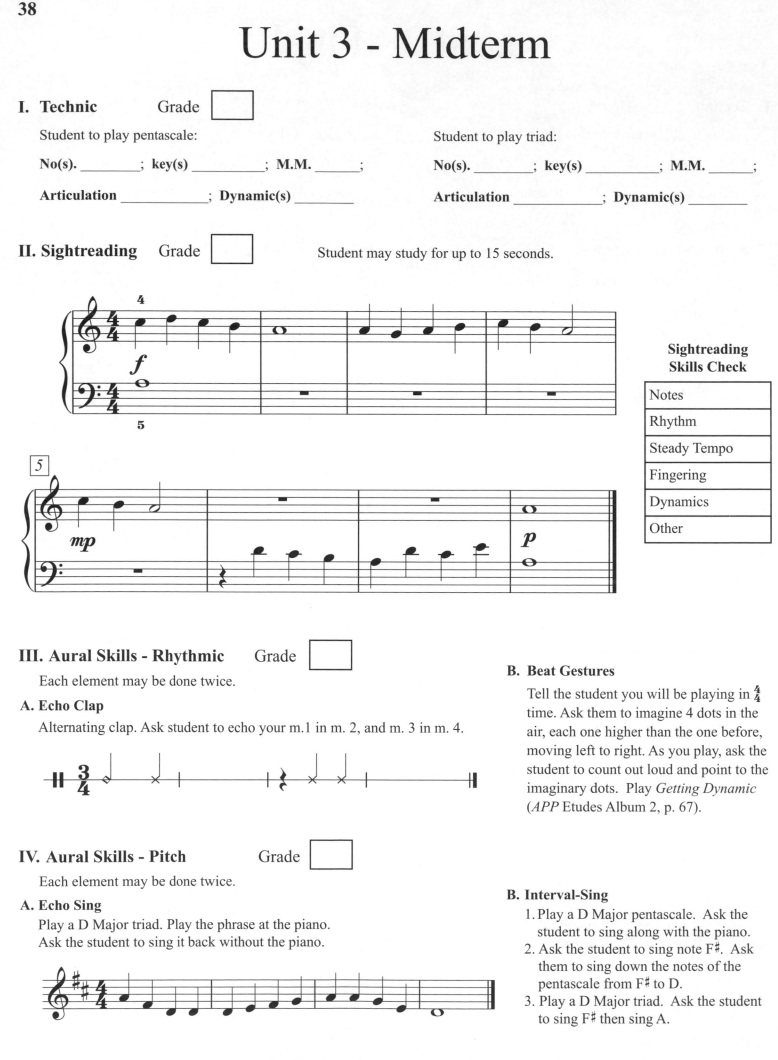

**Sightreading Skills Check**

| Notes |
| Rhythm |
| Steady Tempo |
| Fingering |
| Dynamics |
| Other |

**III. Aural Skills - Rhythmic**    Grade [ ]

Each element may be done twice.

**A. Echo Clap**

Alternating clap. Ask student to echo your m.1 in m. 2, and m. 3 in m. 4.

**B. Beat Gestures**

Tell the student you will be playing in 4/4 time. Ask them to imagine 4 dots in the air, each one higher than the one before, moving left to right. As you play, ask the student to count out loud and point to the imaginary dots. Play *Getting Dynamic* (*APP* Etudes Album 2, p. 67).

**IV. Aural Skills - Pitch**    Grade [ ]

Each element may be done twice.

**A. Echo Sing**

Play a D Major triad. Play the phrase at the piano. Ask the student to sing it back without the piano.

**B. Interval-Sing**

1. Play a D Major pentascale. Ask the student to sing along with the piano.
2. Ask the student to sing note F♯. Ask them to sing down the notes of the pentascale from F♯ to D.
3. Play a D Major triad. Ask the student to sing F♯ then sing A.

# Unit 3 - Final

**I.  Technic**      Grade  [    ]

Student to play pentascale:

No(s). _____ ; key(s) _____ ; M.M. _____ ;

Articulation _____ ; Dynamic(s) _____

Student to play triad:

No(s). _____ ; key(s) _____ ; M.M. _____ ;

Articulation _____ ; Dynamic(s) _____

**II.  Sightreading**      Grade  [    ]      Student may study for up to 15 seconds.

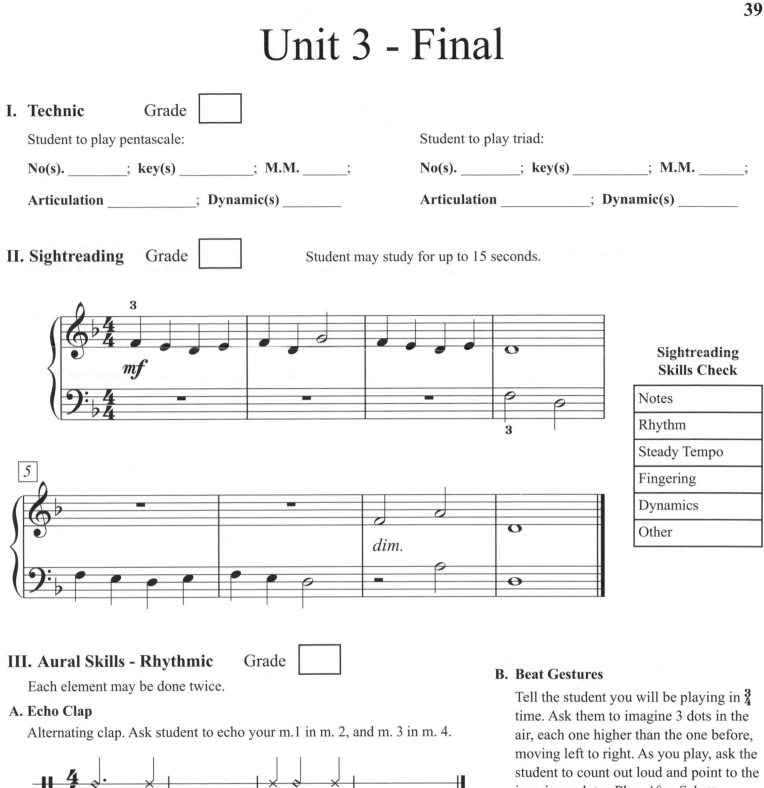

| Sightreading Skills Check |
| --- |
| Notes |
| Rhythm |
| Steady Tempo |
| Fingering |
| Dynamics |
| Other |

**III.  Aural Skills - Rhythmic**      Grade  [    ]

Each element may be done twice.

**A.  Echo Clap**

Alternating clap. Ask student to echo your m.1 in m. 2, and m. 3 in m. 4.

**B.  Beat Gestures**

Tell the student you will be playing in ¾ time. Ask them to imagine 3 dots in the air, each one higher than the one before, moving left to right. As you play, ask the student to count out loud and point to the imaginary dots.  Play *After Schytte* (*APP* Etudes Album 2, p. 62).

**IV.  Aural Skills - Pitch**      Grade  [    ]

Each element may be done twice.

**A.  Echo Sing**

Play a D Major triad. Play the phrase at the piano.
Ask the student to sing it back without the piano.

**B.  Interval-Sing**

1. Play a D Major pentascale.  Ask the student to sing along with the piano.
2. Ask the student to sing note A.  Ask them to sing down the notes of the pentascale from A to D.
3. Play a D Major triad.  Ask the student to sing A then sing F♯.

# Unit 4 - Midterm

**I. Technic**    Grade ☐

Student to play pentascale:

No(s). _____; key(s) _____; M.M. _____;

Articulation _____; Dynamic(s) _____

Student to play triad:

No(s). _____; key(s) _____; M.M. _____;

Articulation _____; Dynamic(s) _____

**II. Sightreading**    Grade ☐    Student may study for up to 15 seconds.

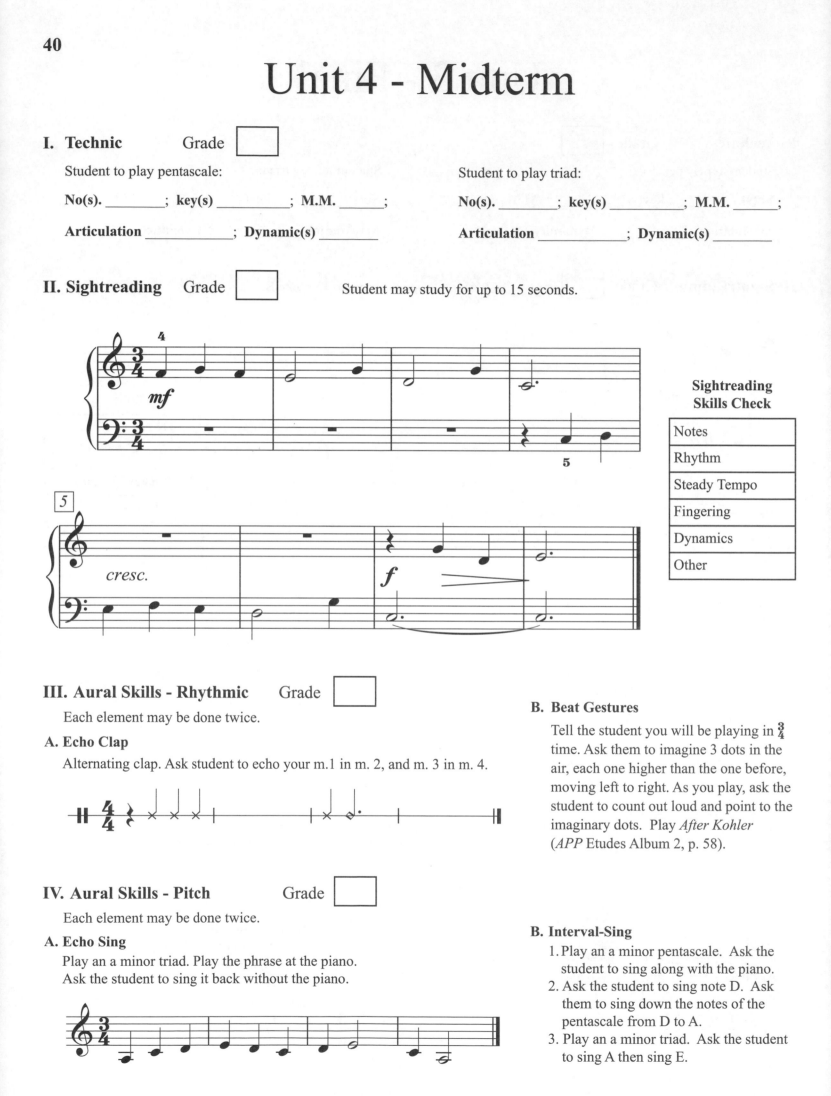

**Sightreading Skills Check**

| Notes |
| --- |
| Rhythm |
| Steady Tempo |
| Fingering |
| Dynamics |
| Other |

**III. Aural Skills - Rhythmic**    Grade ☐

Each element may be done twice.

**A. Echo Clap**

Alternating clap. Ask student to echo your m.1 in m. 2, and m. 3 in m. 4.

**B. Beat Gestures**

Tell the student you will be playing in ¾ time. Ask them to imagine 3 dots in the air, each one higher than the one before, moving left to right. As you play, ask the student to count out loud and point to the imaginary dots.  Play *After Kohler* (*APP* Etudes Album 2, p. 58).

**IV. Aural Skills - Pitch**    Grade ☐

Each element may be done twice.

**A. Echo Sing**

Play an a minor triad. Play the phrase at the piano. Ask the student to sing it back without the piano.

**B. Interval-Sing**

1. Play an a minor pentascale.  Ask the student to sing along with the piano.
2. Ask the student to sing note D.  Ask them to sing down the notes of the pentascale from D to A.
3. Play an a minor triad.  Ask the student to sing A then sing E.

# Unit 4 - Final

**I. Technic**     Grade [ ]

Student to play pentascale:

No(s). _____ ; key(s) _____ ; M.M. _____ ;

Articulation _____ ; Dynamic(s) _____

Student to play triad:

No(s). _____ ; key(s) _____ ; M.M. _____ ;

Articulation _____ ; Dynamic(s) _____

**II. Sightreading**     Grade [ ]     Student may study for up to 15 seconds.

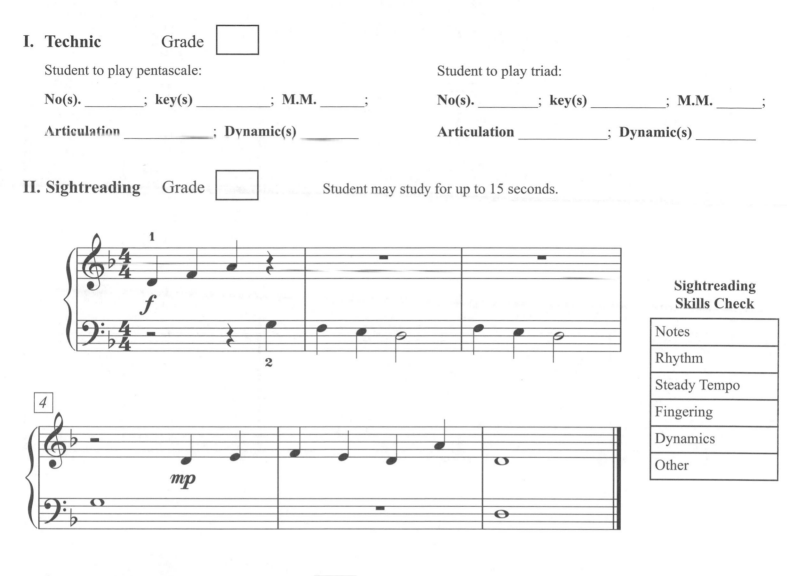

**Sightreading Skills Check**

| Notes |
| Rhythm |
| Steady Tempo |
| Fingering |
| Dynamics |
| Other |

**III. Aural Skills - Rhythmic**     Grade [ ]

Each element may be done twice.

**A. Echo Clap**

Alternating clap. Ask student to echo your m.1 in m. 2, and m. 3 in m. 4.

**B. Beat Gestures**

Tell the student you will be playing in 4/4 time. Ask them to imagine 4 dots in the air, each one higher than the one before, moving left to right. As you play, ask the student to count out loud and point to the imaginary dots. Play *Prairie Song* (*APP* Repertoire Album 2, p. 10).

**IV. Aural Skills - Pitch**     Grade [ ]

Each element may be done twice.

**A. Echo Sing**

Play an a minor triad. Play the phrase at the piano. Ask the student to sing it back without the piano.

**B. Interval-Sing**

1. Play an a minor pentascale. Ask the student to sing along with the piano.
2. Ask the student to sing note E. Ask them to sing down the notes of the pentascale from E to A.
3. Play an a minor triad. Ask the student to sing C then sing A.

# Level 2 Pentascales

No. 1

No. 2

No. 3

No. 4

No. 5

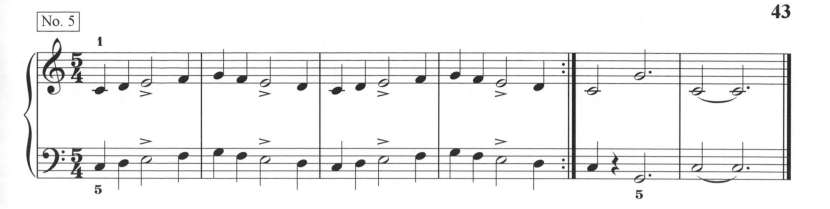

No. 6

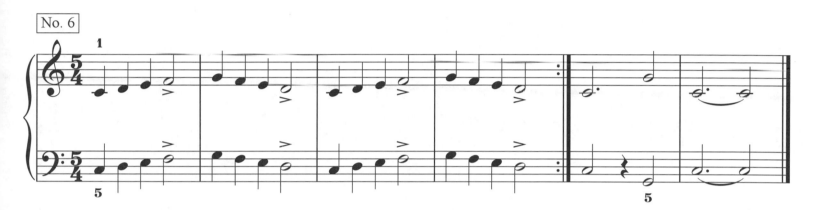

No. 7

No. 8

# Level 2 Triads

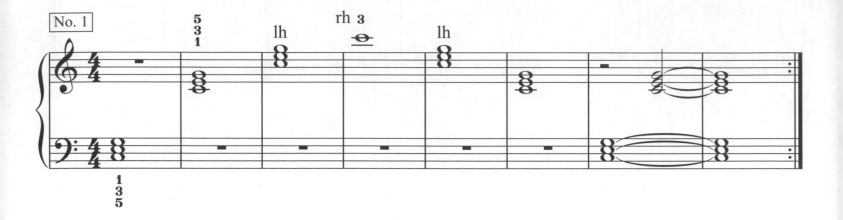

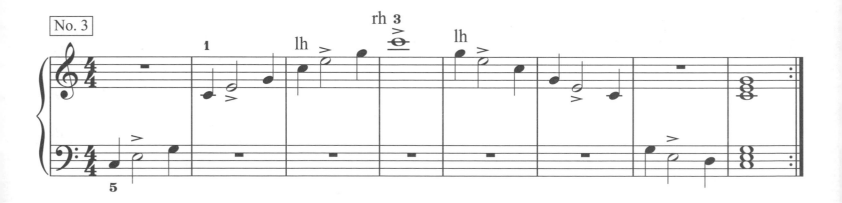

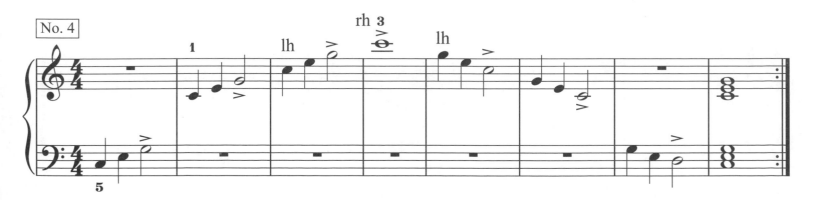

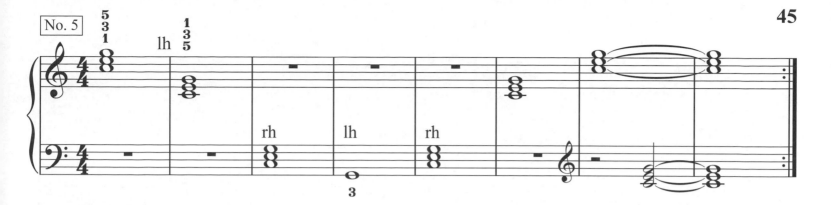

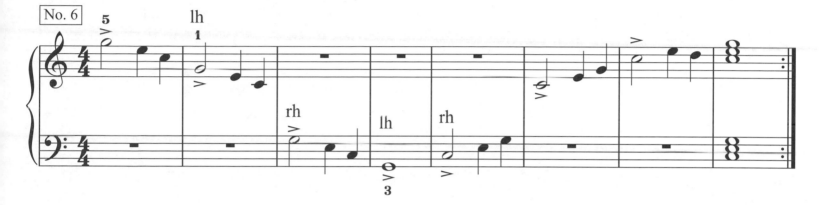

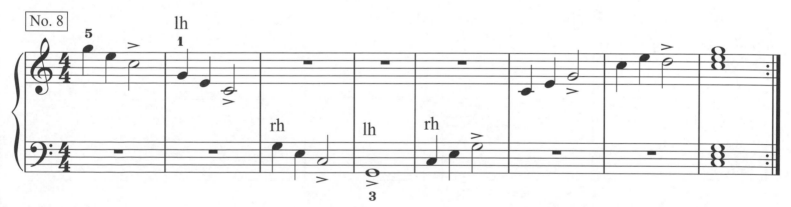

# Level 2 Scale Drills

No. 1

No. 2

No. 3

No. 4

No. 5  *legato*

No. 6  *legato*

48

No. 7

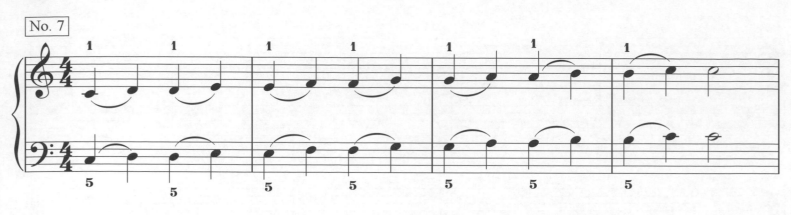

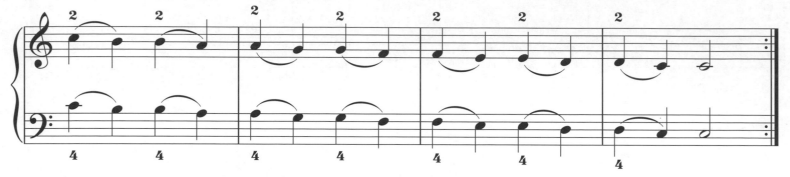

## Fingering Variations

When you are able to play exercise No. 7 with a fluid, even motion, you should move on to the variations on the exercise which use different fingerings in each hand. Do this in each of the assigned keys.

No. 8

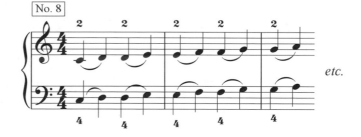

*etc.*

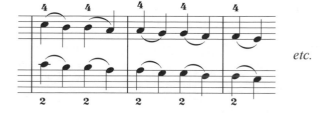

*etc.*

No. 9

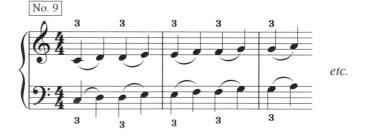

*etc.*

*etc.*

No. 10

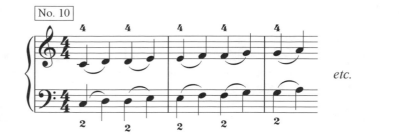

*etc.*

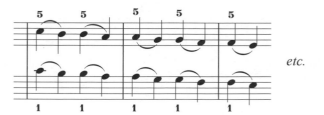

*etc.*

# How to Use This Book

The *American Popular Piano Skills* books are designed to be used as a flexible tool for learning the fundamental skills of playing the piano. Research tells us that the most effective way to learn is in small increments, repeated frequently. That's a good thing, considering that many piano students today have very busy schedules and may not have big chunks of time to devote to practice at one time.

How much time should you spend on basic skills? The best choice, of course, is to spend a moderate amount of time daily on technic, sightreading and ear training. But even a smaller amount of time each day, every day is better than spending a lot of time on one day after several days of non-practice.

## The Open Plan System

The Open Plan organization of the *American Popular Piano Skills* books encourages skill acquisition at each student's natural pace. Review the chart below to help understand how it works.

How should you schedule assignments of Skills? Progress will vary depending on each student's needs and practice timetable.

- **Faster moving students** can do one module per week.
- **Many students** will work on two or three skill areas within a module each week.
- **Students with less practice time** often do just one skill area.

Areas that need extra work may of course be repeated as necessary.

### American Popular Piano
### Skills Book-Level Two

| Four Learning Units to be done by the student at home | | Four Examination Units to be administered by the teacher at the lesson | |
|---|---|---|---|
| **Each Unit contains:** **4 Learning Modules** Each module covers the following skill areas: | | **Each Unit contains:** **2 Tests** **Midterm:** to be completed after Module 2 **Final:** to be completed after Module 4 | |
| **Brainthumpers** | Quick drills on coordination, articulation, grace notes, fingering, and rhythm | **Technic** | Pentascales, triads, and scale preparation |
| **Technic** | Pentascale and triad patterns, and scale preparation to be practiced daily in set keys with a metronome | **Sightreading** | Short examples, with skills checklist |
| **Prepared Sightreading** | A short musical excerpt | **Aural Skills-Rhythmic** | Beat Clap-Along Echo Clap |
| **Aural Skills-Rhythmic** | Clapping (metrical), written work, and echo clapping | **Aural Skills-Pitch** | Interval Sing Echo-Sing |
| **Aural Skills-Pitch** | Triad, interval, and echo singing | | |

## Some Basic Tips

**Singing** Vocalizing has not always been part of traditional piano lessons. Yet recent research has clearly established its importance for developing crucial listening and audiating skills.

Teaching and learning singing in this context is not hard, but does take patience. Many students have not sung and will need some time and work in order to get comfortable. Stick with it! Studies have shown that even those who seem totally tone-deaf on the first attempt can improve significantly with practice.

- Check that posture is good, breathing deep and even, and throat relaxed.
- If the student is having trouble matching pitch, ask them to sing a note and hold it. Find the same pitch and sing it with them. Then ask them to move their voice with you as you sing to the correct pitch.
- Visual and verbal feedback is crucial. Saying "higher" or "lower", or moving your hand up or down to help them find the pitch is a great help.

**Technic** Technic should be practiced daily. Vary the focus of each week's assignment using the Technic Box in each Module.

- **Fill in the blanks** for the metronome marking (M.M.) and the number of the exercise.
- **Circle** the chosen key(s), articulation(s), and dynamic(s).

Technical exercises are set out in C Major in the last few pages of this book. For students who work better from a printed page, consider using the *Level 2 Technic Book* for the other keys.

**Sightreading** The word "sightreading" is a misnomer; a better term might be "pattern recognition" or even "flash learning". A good sightreader recognizes familiar patterns in new arrangements; he or she is able to think ahead, keep going despite mistakes, and keep a steady beat.

Here are some steps that have helped my students improve their sightreading:

- Play the piece at a slow tempo without stopping. After finishing, go back and circle mistakes. This builds both analysis and musical memory skills.
- Play slowly again and try to fix all the mistakes – and not add any new ones!
- Play a third time, counting out loud. This time it should be error free.

Steps may be repeated as necessary.

**Mix** Do you have to do all the activities for every section? You'll make the right decision based on available time, skill level and long-term goals. Remember, the most important factor in improving fundamentals is: **work on them — and do it often!!**